Down in the Bottom

of the Bottom

of the Box

DOWN IN THE BOTTOM OF THE BOTTOM OF THE BOX

JONARNO LAWSON

Paper Cuts by Alec Dempster

The Porcupine's Quill

Library and Archives Canada Cataloguing in Publication

Lawson, JonArno
    Down in the bottom of the bottom of the box / JonArno Lawson;
paper cuts by Alec Dempster.

Poems.
ISBN 978-0-88984-354-7

    I. Dempster, Alec, 1971– II. Title.

PS8573.A93D68 2012   jc811'.54   C2012-904783-X

Published by The Porcupine's Quill, 68 Main Street, PO Box 160,
Erin, Ontario NOB ITO. http://porcupinesquill.ca

Represented in Canada by the Literary Press Group.
Trade orders are available from University of Toronto Press.

We acknowledge the support of the Ontario Arts Council and the
Canada Council for the Arts for our publishing program. The finan-
cial support of the Government of Canada through the Canada Book
Fund is also gratefully acknowledged.

For Lissa Paul & Michael Joseph &
Sophie, Ashey, Joseph, Sam, Jacob, & Zoe

Poor little Tom without a bubble
sunk beneath the waves.
Happy Ginny with a bottle of gin
and a cork to keep Tom's spirit in.

— Michael Joseph

If I were you and you were me
And we all set out to go to sea
How many of us would there be?

— Jean Lawson Buck Valeruso

Our Imaginary Selves

'I'm sorry,' Noah said, 'we've taken all that we can carry,
God never said I could save anyone imaginary ...'
'Don't worry,' said the gryphon to the downcast dwarves and elves,
'we'll build another ark for our imaginary selves.'

The Golden Calf

Aaron shrugged while Moses snapped,
'Enough of your tomfoolery!'
Shamefaced, the former slaves transformed their calf
back into jewellery.

8

Daniel in the Lions' Den

'Don't eat him,' said the mother lion.
'Do now as I bid. If we leave him
they might bring us more
than just this scrawny kid.'

People Through a Peephole

See the people
through a peephole
down a steep hole
from a steeple.

The Solar Bears

The Solar Bears
strike fast and bright
and dynamite the skies –
to strip away your vision
and repopulate your eyes

with fortress-featured
furnaced layers
of giant
sun-furred
solar bears.

The world
that they incinerate's
a roaring mane of light
what they don't
blast apart by day
they detonate
by night.

It will take you aeons to
recuperate your sight.

12

Lunar Foxes

The lunar foxes left the moon
but left without direction
to slip beyond all telescopic
methods of detection

(but that's just like the fox
who deals in dodges
and deception,
oh yes, how like the fox).

Perhaps they orbit round some
distant planet far away
or simply sniff and dip and drift
around the Milky Way;

to find them now you'll need
your extrasensory perception:
your mind, if your mind talks to you,
will hook up the connection

to some freewheeling,
comet-stealing
double-dealing
lunar fox.

14

Moonwolves

Moonwolves howl in harmony at earth,
the sun's blue moon.
But here on earth the earthwolves howl
in and out of tune.

An awful conversation.

Moonwolves smoulder over
broken slopes and giant dunes:
in weightless lunar-lupine hearts
they long for other moons.

Harmonized
and hard at work,
ignoring all temptation,
ready to explore,

loping to our cloudy door
while earthwolves whimper
listlessly and long
for a vacation.

Goose

The goose that lays a golden egg –
it's quite a trick to catch it.
But once a golden egg's been laid
the greater trick's to hatch it.

Beautiful Insomniac

After Sleeping Beauty woke, she never slept again;
she feared another fairy attack,
and that's why Sleeping Beauty's now
a beautiful insomniac.

Baa, Baa

'Baa, baa, black sheep,
have you any wool?'
'No,' said the black sheep,
and gave your nose a pull.

The Tree and the Telephone Pole

A tree stood next to a telephone pole and said,
'I've just detected: your branches and your roots are gone,
not only that, your bark's not on!
Poor tree, so disrespected!'
The telephone pole reflected:
'It's true in a way, you're very astute,
I lack branches, bark and root,
but I'm still held in high repute,
because I'm well connected.'

Snow White

If you don't know where it's from, be careful,
don't succumb – check it with your thumb.
If its origins are unknown, don't sit with it on your own,
or hang about or linger, probe it with your finger.
If its provenance is indeterminate, better look for a worm in it.
And if you still don't know, inspect it with your toe.

Little Red Riding Wolf

The little dog growled,
the dish divorced the spoon,
when Little Red Riding Wolf
howled at the moon.

20

The Bottom of the Box

Down in the bottom of the bottom of the box
dig a little deeper – those aren't socks.
Here come the teeth of a hungry fox
jumping up your arm like electric shocks.

The Top

When speaking of the top is it
the bottom that's the opposite?
Or is it what we find above
the top we should be speaking of?

The Truth

There is an important truth;
that seems both consistent and constant to me:
the truth is that the truth is never
what anybody wants it to be.

Leaping, Creeping, Sheep and Sleeping

Turtles have creep overs,
Frogs have leap overs,
Goats have sheep over,
Sloths have sleepovers.

Convincing Contradictions

Unpredictable predictions.
Hospitable evictions.
Affable afflictions.
Adaptable addictions.

Unconstrained restrictions.
Ambivalent convictions.
Void-of-form depictions.
Convincing contradictions.

Tight-fisted generosity.
Indifferent curiosity.
Affectionate animosity.
Beautiful monstrosity.

Lambs and Rams in Traffic Jams

Lambs and rams in traffic jams bleat instead of beeping.
The mildness of their demands condemns them to go creeping
with cars while kangaroos pass by
intuitively leaping.

Ostrich

An ostrich stretches its head over hedges
and leaps over ditches
to add to the riches
it robs from the wretches fate fetches,
dredges
and drops
off ledges
or hitches
to the edges of the lands
where he's bound.
And some say he wedges
his head in the ground
when unnerved.
And in this way alleges
his head can't be found,
poor bird.
But that isn't right –
it's a false accusation.
He's just flipping his eggs
from the top of his legs
doing his bit
when he's sick of the sit
for the chicks' gestation.

A Budgie in a Buggy

A budgie in a buggy had a buddy with a grudge:
a toucan in a moving van had given him a nudge.
He nudged him back and nipped him,
but the toucan wouldn't budge.
Which one was less commendable?
It's up to you to judge.

Blubbery Bears

Blubbery bears
eating blueberries bear
the weight of their blubber
with barely a care.

Greenblatt, Goldblatt, Grenby, Grinch

Greenblatt, Goldblatt, Grenby, Grinch.
Schoolyard, scrapyard, inchworm, inch.
Obadiah would you try a little bitta jumbalaya?
Spoonful, capful, peanut-butter pinch!

Monkeys in the Dump

A clump of clumsy monkeys lumbered through the dump.
The clumsiest amongst them tumbled over in the junk –
it jumped and spun and tried to run but crumpled to its rump
then slunk away until it slumped into the muck, and sunk.

The Human Being

Bombard its brain with cosmic rays.
redden its eyes with Mars –
set its tiny heart ablaze
upon a heap of stars.

Astronaut

I asked her not
to say astronaut.
She said, 'Astronaut –
sorry – I forgot!'

Remember Where You Were?

Remember where you were?
Look where you are now:
you got here half by guessing well,
and half by asking how.

A Coarse and Common Carrot

I'll tell you of a coarse and common carrot I once knew;
unwashed, unpeeled, impatient with what vegetables must do,
she crept up to the pot and cried, 'Goodbye now, toodle-oo!':
then with a hop she dropped herself unchopped into the stew.

The Chilly Sicken

The chilly sicken
because they're cold,
and the silly chicken
won't do as it's told!

The Mansarumé Fish

It seems when you eat a Mansarumé fish
you at once become hopelessly stuck
with this sad and unfortunate state of affairs:
when you eat it, you get its bad luck.

There Are Things That You Face

There are things that you face with your face,
and things that you face with your rear.
There are things that you face all over the place,
and things that you face only here.
You may face things with courage or face things with fear,
sunk in depression or full of good cheer,
with a semblance of grace, or a plastic veneer,
but never face life with a sneer.

A Cock Can Crow

A cock can crow, but a crow can't cock.
A macaw can't caw but it sure can squawk.
Let a mockingbird mock at the call of an auk
but a caw's the law when crows talk.

The Stickler and the Slacker

The stickler and the slacker were niggling over nickels –
the slacker had a knack for getting sticklers into pickles:
the stickler told the slacker he should find another backer,
but the slacker said he wouldn't, and he ate the stickler's cracker.

The Sun

It rises up ferocious –
swinging swords of yellow light –
sinks gory orange and smouldering,
it rolls into the night.

Burning Hot Banana

I bought a burning hot banana from a bin in Indiana
with a burning hot and sticky splitting freckly yellow skin –
splotchy-rotten overripe – thick enough to clog a pipe –
when I think of it today I sweat and sicken from within.

During the Week

During the week he never felt weak
but on the weekend he weakened,
when his sense of being weak-kneed
deepened.

36

Agony

When he fell from his wagon he
roared out in agony.
Any small hurt made him
dreadfully dragony.

Recommend

What do you recommend,
wreck or mend?
What do your suggest?
(Don't answer, it's a jest.)

Axe

An axe cracks the old tree-backs
and bark begins to fly:
I've got slivers and chips on my tongue and my lips
and a splinter in my eye.

Baburnama Kalevala

Baburnama Kalevala
Gesta Romanorum
Panchatantra Shahnameh
Jataka Kathasaritsagara!

Identity

Welsh fingers and Scottish toes –
Irish eyes and an English nose:
I'm a Brit – every bit of me's a Brit from Britain –
and the parts of me that aren't have to fight to fit in.

Twins

When you're a twin, your life begins at once with twice the force.
You're plunked in bunks, you ride a double-decker rocking horse.
The trouble is what can be doubled can just as well be cut in half –
and when that happens twins don't laugh.
They sober up at once, of course.

The Alleycat Alley-allocator
Acting Like an Alligator

He's a catastrophic caterwauler,
cruelly clawed and callous –
lacking principles or pity;
fetid, flawed and full of malice
but very, very pretty in a kitty sort of way.
Although you feel like saying
'It's an alley, not a palace that you're allocating,
kitty, to the other alley cats.'

A Second Water Waltz

Look how your lovely face exalts,
when you forget about my faults:
suddenly, accepting me,
your lovely face reflecting me – up you spring –
your body vaults, and diving in with somersaults
you find the surface of my skin,
and join me in my water waltz.

44

Preposterous Fossils

'Look at these preposterous fossils I dug up last week!'
'Not fossils, sir – they're ostrich nostrils, in an ostrich beak!'
Astonished, he returned them to the ostrich he'd aggrieved:
the ostrich he returned them to was very much relieved.

Does Rita Eat a Pita?

Does Rita eat a pita,
while Nitza eats a pizza?
Did Nikita meet Anita?
Did a cheetah cheat a cheetah?

Push-Broom Bum

He had a bike-chain spine and a push-broom bum,
and a hollow where he'd wallow till the wassailers would come,
with their cider pots, and their tunes to hum –
then he'd crawl out of his crater with his bougarabou drum.

I Broke the Bones of One O'Clock

I tried to gather time, a second at a time –
but when the clock began to chime
it poured the seconds out. I broke the bones
of one o'clock and hid them in my father's sock,
but when he pulled his stocking on,
he said, 'What's this in here, my son?
What are you doing with your time?
Don't waste it, precious one.'

The Fortitor and Fidelitor

The Fortitor and Fidelitor of the First
(and the final) Funicular
was on his way to do nothing at all
(or at least nothing in particular).
The rain when it fell, he noted quite well,
fell pear-shaped and perpendicular
while out in the street he could see, through the sleet,
that the traffic was all vehicular.

Seize the Day

The sensible day
will bite the hand that seizes it –
and the sensible hand
will find some briefer moment that pleases it.

I Played with Toys

I played with toys, and later,
I learned to play inside them.
Inside them was the only way to keep them,
because I couldn't find a way to hide them.
While inside them, I learned to play without them
and within them (so without them)
I no longer thought about them.

Robot Bones

I swore an oath, a solemn oath,
that I would bury the bones of both,
side by side together,
in the crackling electrical undergrowth
(a final nest of red-hot wires wrapped them in their tomb).
I swore to them by the ozone layer
(back in the days when it was still there),
and we all knelt down
for a digital prayer,
while a fleeting memory saddened me
of his tungsten hand on her copper hair.

Dadder Dan

There never was a badder man
than that nasty Dadder Dan –
he's digging back into your past he's
digging up fantastic nasties.

Ping Molly

Ping Molly, Ping Molly, Molly Molly Ping.
Scrawl a note to Molly on a jackdaw's wing.
If Molly answers, write her back again –
ask her why and where and how, but never ask her when.

The Minimum Amount of Money

What's the minimum amount of money, Mum?
A minimal amount is a criminal sum –
subliminally small – slightly more than none,
that's the minimum amount of money, son.

Otis

Otis, I notice your boat is afloat is
your boat as afloat as a toad in a moat is?
I hope not! I said to him. While most boats float
most toads can't swim.

Audrey and Aubrey

Aubrey and Audrey were quite a pair –
oddly Audrey was never there.
Aubrey was; she left him waiting,
though he found it irritating.

Gingerbread Injury

It's easy to injure a gingerbread man
and a gingerbread injury's bound to expand
from a foot to a leg from a head to a hand
when you're eating him, eating him, fast as you can.

A Lazy Baby Ladybug

A lazy baby ladybug
fell like a little drop of blood.
Another fell, another fell:
drip, click, swarm and swell.

Jispering Whibberish

Those who whisper jibberish
may end up jispering whibberish –
or blathering rubbishy jibber-jabber,
or nattering noisome blibber-blabber.

56

Octopus

An octopus spots an illusory obstacle, unfurls a tentacle,
chops with a popsicle. Obstinate octopus! Awkward, impractical.
(Popsicle chopping is slow and suboptimal
when the illusion you're chopping is optical.)

This Word

This word was misheard.
This word was mis-sbelled.
And this word was *whispered*.
And this word was YELLED.

Solitary Tennis

The racquet whacked at an ordinary ball
in a parking lot, at a concrete wall –
it popped, dropped, another hard chop –
ricochet, Bombay, bounce and plop.

The Deep End

How deep the deep end is depends
on how deep down
the deep end ends
and where the shallow end begins.

Ought a Taught Rat to Gnaw at a Taut Knot?

A rat gnawed at a knot, just as it was taught.
Is that odd or ought a rat to ignore a knot that's taut?
Whether you nod or not
I hope that rat gets caught.

He Breaks Away

He breaks away –
runs up the hill –
the world is his.

Why does he stop –
peer back?
Stand still,

ears lifted? No?
Keep going?
Is getting caught

by an eye
like this, like that,
the thrill?

The greatest thrill?
I'll bet it is –
to writhe

and slither
and slide
away –

to run
take shelter
and hide away.

And then? What then?
He turns about and begs
for his dependence,

who just a moment back
had been transcendence
on two legs.

Directions

First	way	sharp	end.
down	this	right	the
this	up	down	left,
way	then	again	sharp

Ma, Pa, Oops-a-Lah! (A Culinary Brouhaha)

Ma, Pa, oops-a-lah!
Put it in the oven but it comes out raw –
See saw, oom-pah-pah.
Put it back in, Mama – ooh-la-la!

Woulda Coulda Shoulda, Didn't

Woulda coulda shoulda didn't –
wouldja couldja shouldja now?
Willya wontcha? Ifya dontcha'll
get it someday anyhow.

Night Kite

May by day, might by night,
do by dark, don't by light.
Tie it, fly it, flip in flight –
hello yellow black and white.

Forgiving and Forgetting

I've found a way of living
half the time for giving
but when I start regretting
giving, then I live for getting.

Beliefs

Conflicting beliefs
so busy colliding
have no time to conquer –
they're too busy dividing.

Fragile's Fragility

FRAGILE: drop G and drop E
the word becomes FRAIL,
then drop out the R
to see the word FAIL.

A's and O's

You read your a's and o's
with ease
but didn't use
your eyes.

First He Was Thirsty

First he was thirsty
second he beckoned
the third with a word
while the fourth went forth.

Double You

You may think there's just one you
If so, I hate to trouble you –
But just in case you didn't know

You're actually a **W**.

Mother Snake

The mother snake said, 'Daughter dear,
you know I'd never mislead you:
do what's right – never bite –
but hiss whenever you need to.'

Little Piggies

This little piggy went to park it,
and this little piggy paid the fare.
This little piggy pawed the carpet,
but this little piggy didn't dare.
And the last little piggy went wee
wee wee to Wawa in a mobile home.

Flies Flee Fred's French Fries Franchise

Why's the fly Fred fed surprised?
Well-fed flies fled Fred's
French fries franchise
because every fly that Fred feeds dies.

Dizzy, Drifting

Dizzy, drifting hither thither,
dillydally dawdle dither –
lurk and lay about and linger – loiter and delay,
lollygag and loaf around, and lounge away the day.

Lift Her Aloft

Lift her aloft! (her laughter left her) –
her foot's soft! (you have to heft her) –
up on a rafter, follow her after –
though dippy, she's defter – though dopey, you're dafter.

Michael and Mike

You can tell the second you meet them
the moment you see what they're like:
Mike's more a Mike than a Michael –
Michael's more Michael than Mike.

You can run again through the whole cycle
as often and much as you like:
Mike's more a Mike than a Michael
Michael's more Michael than Mike.

Take a last look, and look closely
I'm sure you will see that I'm right:
it will strike you that Mike is no Michael,
and also that Michael's no Mike.

Who Did I Write This For?

For M., who'll never see it.
For J., who didn't want it.
For F., who'll never read it.
For X., who wouldn't need it.

A Kitty Cat a Cookie and a Can of Coca-Cola

A kitty cat a cookie and a can of Coca-Cola.
A kitty cat a cookie and a can of Coca-Cola.
She used her paw to hold her straw
to sip her Coca-Cola

because she didn't like the feel of bubbles on her whiskers –
of bubbles on her whiskers!
but I was told in whispers
I wasn't told aloud

and so it's very possible
that she wasn't proud, of her insipid sipping
but her straw was not withdrawn
the last time that I saw her, though her soda pop was gone.

Underneath the School

Just underneath the school there's often clay
and slugs and sand, and battle-broken bones,
a baby's beads and old corn-grinding stones –
who knows what else lies underneath the school?

Dig deeper down through layers and layers of crust,
down through the mantle's hidden veins of ore
beyond the heat's too awful to ignore –
like you yourself, earth has a molten core.

Eunice's Unicycle

Icicles hung from Eunice's unicycle.
Michael said, 'Eunice?' Eunice said, 'Yes, Michael?'
'Eunice, as soon as the moon is bright,
let's ride your unicycle out into the night.'
'All right,' said Eunice. 'The moon is bright!' –
and so she and Michael softly unicycled out of sight.

Acknowledgements

Thank you to the Canada Council, the Grant for Professional Writers program, for a grant towards this book's completion.

Thanks to Robert Twigger, who suggested Lunar Foxes and Moonwolves as possible companions for Solar Bears, and to Lissa Paul and Michael Joseph for their tireless support and encouragement through many early versions.

Thank you to the following publications (and their editors): *This Book Makes No Sense* (Michael Heyman), *The Scrumbler* (Michael Kavanagh), *Read Me at School* (Gaby Morgan), IBBY's *Book Bird* and ALA's *Book Links* (Sylvia Vardell), Gottabook.blogspot.com (Greg Pincus), and *Poetryzone* (James Pickersgill) for publishing many of these poems first.

Sheila Barry provided enormous encouragement with this book (and its twin sister, *Think Again*) from the very beginning. Anne Green, at Wordfest in Calgary, allowed me the opportunity of a live audience to use as a laboratory.

Amy – my dear wife – came up with the line 'Fred's French fries franchise' in a car outside Harbord Bakery (of all the unfranchise-like places)! Also, the phrase 'push-broom bum'. Sophie was the source of the name 'Dadder Dan', Ashey came up with the idea of a double-decker rocking horse, Joseph inspired the line 'minimum amount of money, Mum?' with the miniminiminimum sound he used to make. 'Our Imaginary Selves' was directly based on a conversation between Sophie and Ashey back in 2007 during which they came up with the concept, the vocabulary, and even a first draft. Theirs also is the phrase 'peanut-butter pinch'.

The MacFarlanes, of Fiona's Bake Shop and Tea Room in Wasaga Beach, and Liza Hardoon of To Go, on Yonge Street in Toronto, created perfect destinations to work in.

Michelle Walker pointed out the artistic genius of Alec Dempster. I'm extremely grateful to Tim and Elke Inkster for their belief and investment in my work, and in this project. I also wanted to thank Kathleen Icely and Doris Cowan for their indispensable help.

My Aunt Jean wrote 'If I were you and you were me' when she had young children, back in the 1940s and '50s. Michael Joseph's 'Poor little Tom without a bubble' is used without his permission, to surprise him. Second Walter Waltz is a revision of an earlier version that appears in *Black Stars in a White Night Sky*. I discovered the Mansarumé fish in Sebastian Hope's amazing *Outcasts of the Islands*.

JonArno Lawson is a two-time winner of the Lion and the Unicorn Award for Excellence in North American Poetry. His most recent books were *There Devil, Eat That* and *Old MacDonald Had Her Farm*. He lives in Toronto with his wife, Amy, and three children, Sophie, Ashey, and Joseph.

Alec Dempster was born in Mexico City in 1971 but moved to Toronto as a child. In 1995 he returned to Mexico, and settled in Xalapa, Veracruz, where his relief prints eventually became infused with the local tradition of *son jarocho* music. Alec's conversations with rural musicians, presented along with thirty linoleum portraits, have been published recently as *Faces and Voices of Son Jarocho*. He has produced six CDs of son jarocho recorded in the field, but is perhaps best known for his two lotería games – El Fandanguito-Lotería de Sones Jarochos and the Lotería Huasteca – which include over a hundred prints. Alec now lives in Toronto. His own son jarocho group Café Con Pan has released two albums, a self-titled debut, and the recent *Nuevos Caminos a Santiago*, which are available at www.cafeconpan.ca.